MW01114506

AMELIA EARHART

Gloria D. Miklowitz

Dominie Press, Inc.

Publisher: Raymond Yuen
Editor: John S. F. Graham
Designer: Greg DiGenti
Photo Credits: Bettmann/Corbis (pages 6, 8, 12, 17, 26, and cover); Underwood and Underwood/ Corbis (pages 15 and 19); Corbis (page 23)

Published by:

℗ Dominie Press, Inc.

1949 Kellogg Avenue
Carlsbad, California 92008 USA

www.dominie.com

Paperback ISBN 0-7685-1213-1
Library Bound Edition ISBN 0-7685-1538-6
Printed in Singapore by PH Productions Pte Ltd
2 3 4 5 6 PH 04 03

Table of Contents

Chapter 1
Taking Risks 5

Chapter 2
Only a Toothbrush 11

Chapter 3
Flying Was Fun 16

Chapter 4
New Records 21

Chapter 5
A Mystery 25

Glossary 30

Taking Risks

Amelia Earhart was born in Atchison, Kansas in 1897. At that time, most people had never even seen a car. Airplanes didn't exist yet.

She and her little sister, Muriel, grew up in Atchison with their grandparents.

Their parents moved often because their father, a lawyer for many different railroads, took jobs in different cities. It wasn't until Amelia was 12 that the two girls went to live permanently with their parents in Des Moines, Iowa.

When Amelia Earhart was six years old, in 1903, the Wright brothers built and flew the first powered airplane. Its longest flight lasted 59 seconds.

The Wright brothers' first flight

At the 1904 World's Fair in St. Louis, Missouri, a cash prize was offered to anyone who could fly for 10 minutes.

People were fascinated with flying. Some jumped off barn roofs, holding parachutes that looked like umbrellas. Others sailed off hills on gliders, hoping the wind would carry them.

Amelia saw her first airplane at the Iowa State Fair in Des Moines, but she was impressed with roller coasters, not airplanes. Back home, she tried to build a roller coaster. She attached wheels to a board and built the track out of wooden planks. The "track" went down from the top of a shed. She rode her roller coaster again and again, despite a few crash landings. "It's like flying!" she shouted. Always adventurous, Amelia felt that taking risks was fun.

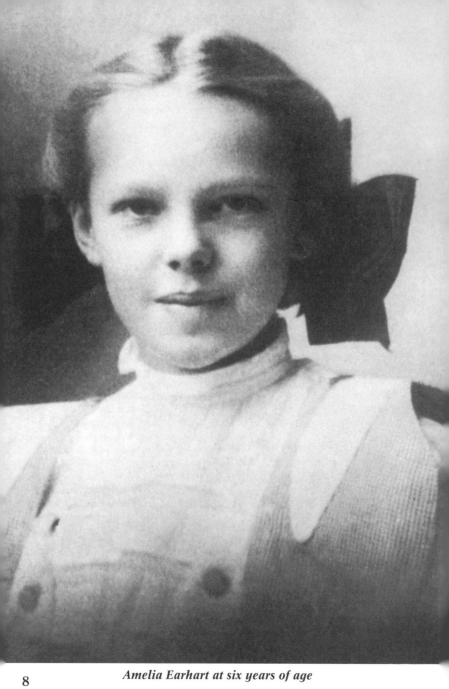

Amelia Earhart at six years of age

Amelia's childhood was happy. With her younger sister, she caught bugs, rode bicycles, and played sports. In high school, she did well in chemistry and physics. She attended college but did not finish. Instead, she worked as a volunteer nurse during World War I.

One day, Amelia watched an air show in the Los Angeles area. Her father paid $1 for her to take her first flight. Right away, Amelia fell in love with flying. She asked for $1,000 to take lessons. "I can't afford that," her father said.

Amelia worked at many jobs to pay for lessons. She cut her long, blond hair and began wearing old army clothes like men pilots. By her 24th birthday, she had passed her pilot's test to get a license. Her mother and sister helped her buy a small plane for her birthday. She painted it yellow and called it *The Canary*. She was one of only a few women to have a pilot's license at that time.

She spent the next several years as a teacher and social worker in Boston. She still loved flying, but she couldn't earn a living at it. She flew airplanes in her spare time and spent what little money she had helping to promote flying for women pilots.

Chapter 2

Only a Toothbrush

One day Amelia received an interesting phone call. The caller said, "Would you be interested in doing something for aviation? It could be dangerous." Charles Lindbergh had flown alone over the Atlantic Ocean just a few months before—something

The Friendship *on its transatlantic flight*

no one had ever done. The caller asked
if Amelia would be willing to fly across
the Atlantic. She would be the first
woman to do so.

On June 18, 1928, on an airplane
named *Friendship*, she took off from
Newfoundland, Canada. The *Friendship*
was painted bright orange and had
pontoons so it could land on water.
It also had extra fuel tanks, which
replaced the seats. Amelia crouched

behind the pilot to record the flight. Because she was not licensed for instrument flying, Bill Stultz piloted the plane. "There is nothing to see but churned mist, very white in the afternoon sun," she wrote.

Twenty hours and 40 minutes after takeoff, they landed on water near a little town in England. Amelia waved a white towel out the window to get attention. A man on shore removed his shirt and waved back. Finally, someone came for them.

Crowds cheered everywhere. People sent Amelia clothes when they learned she had taken only a toothbrush along. President Calvin Coolidge sent his congratulations. Amelia felt she had received more credit than she deserved. She sent a message back, saying, "Success entirely due to Mr. Stultz."

When Amelia returned to the United States, George Putnam of the Putnam publishing family suggested that she write a book. Putnam taught her how to talk to audiences so she could promote it. Her book, *20 Hrs. 40 Min.* sold well. During that same year she became the first person to fly alone from the East Coast to the West Coast of the United States.

In 1929, she bought a Lockheed Vega and flew it in the first Women's Air Derby. Her plane finished third. There were many good female pilots, but Putnam's publicity skills helped make Amelia the most well-known of them all.

"Women should be able to seek, as men, any gainful occupation their talents and interests make available," Amelia said.

*Amelia Earhart prepares for the
first Women's Air Derby*

Chapter 3

Flying Was Fun

Amelia married George Putnam
in 1931, after his sixth proposal. She
wrote him that she intended to
continue doing things that meant a lot
to her. She said that neither one of
them should interfere with each other's
work or play.

Amelia Earhart and her husband, George Putnam

After her marriage, Amelia set an altitude record flying an autogiro, an aircraft that is half airplane and half helicopter. She flew it cross-country while advertising chewing gum on the airplane's side.

Flying was always fun for Amelia. In the previous four years, she had flown solo nearly 1,000 hours, many of which she flew on instruments. She would need those skills. One day she asked her husband, "Would you mind if I flew across the Atlantic?" He agreed and had her red Vega outfitted with a new engine and extra gas tanks.

On May 19, 1932 good weather was predicted for the flight. Amelia rushed home to get her helmet, leather jacket and pants, a toothbrush, and $15. She flew to Newfoundland first, taking off across the Atlantic from there.

Earhart tests an autogiro

During the flight, her altimeter failed, so she couldn't tell how high she was flying. Ice formed on the plane's wings and windshield. To melt it, Amelia dove so low, she could see the ocean waves. The plane climbed into fog and storms. One of the engines caught fire, but Amelia didn't have enough fuel to turn back.

About 15 hours after takeoff, Amelia landed in Northern Ireland in a grassy pasture. It was five years to the day after Lindbergh's acclaimed solo flight. He sent his congratulations.

The world went wild. "Not Americans only, not women only, but the whole world is proud of her," wrote *The London Times*. France awarded Amelia the Cross of the Legion of Honor. The United States gave her the Distinguished Flying Cross. Amelia said, "It proved to me and to everyone else that a woman... could do it."

Chapter 4

New Records

Amelia gave talks at breakfasts, luncheons, and teas all over the country to earn money for more flights.

She set new records: Los Angeles to Newark, New Jersey—nonstop—in 19 hours and five minutes. (Today,

this flight would take a little over
five hours.)

In 1933, she came in third in an
air race against mostly male fliers,
cutting two hours off her Los Angeles-
to-Newark record.

By 1934, Navy pilots were flying
planes from California to Hawaii.
Amelia decided to do the reverse and fly
from Hawaii to California. It would be
"easier to hit a continent than an
island," she said. Ten people had lost
their lives flying that same route, and
no one had ever attempted it alone.

George Putnam made sure that two
altimeters and more gas tanks were
put in Amelia's new Lockheed Vega.
A 2-foot-long route map was prepared.
A radio, rubber raft, hatchet, and

Well-wishers greet Earhart upon the completion of her historic flight from Hawaii to California

knife were included—safety equipment that had not been on her previous Atlantic flight.

Amelia and her husband sailed to Hawaii with the Vega aboard the ship. Few people knew of her plans. On the morning of Jan. 11, 1935, gale-force winds blew and rain poured down, but in early afternoon the sky cleared. Amelia had to leave quickly before another storm arrived from the west.

Amelia flew nonstop—2,400 miles—in 18 hours and 15 minutes. *The New York Times* wrote: "Out of the wind and rain-whipped Pacific, Amelia Earhart landed in Oakland, California, at 1:31 p.m., California time." Her flight was considered as historic as that of Lindbergh's. She was now the first to fly across both the Atlantic and Pacific oceans, and the first to fly solo over the Pacific. She had one more record to set—a flight that would take her around the world.

Chapter 5

A Mystery

Amelia, nearly 40 years old, had a new plane—a Lockheed Electra. It had two engines and many extras, including new direction-finding equipment.

Others had already flown around the world, but at its narrowest points—

Earhart and Fred Noonan discuss their flight around the world

near the North and South Poles. Amelia wanted to circle the world at its widest point—the equator. Her plan was to fly west from California.

George got permission from all the countries she would fly over, and arranged for gas and spare parts to be at each stop. Amelia flew first to Hawaii. On March 11, she took off from Pearl Harbor, Hawaii with Fred Noonan, her navigator, and Paul Mantz, who knew Morse code. Heavily loaded with fuel, the Electra belly-flopped, damaging its wings. "I don't know what happened," Amelia said.

The Electra was sent to California for repairs.

Amelia still wanted to make the journey, but she decided to fly east, instead. This time, the only other person in the plane was Noonan, the navigator. They left Miami on June 1, 1937. The flight took them down the coast of South America, to Africa, India, Singapore, Australia, and Lae, New Guinea—more than 25 stops.

The plan was to fly every day, but there were many delays because of repairs or bad weather. From Lae, the most dangerous leg of the trip lay ahead—a 2,556-mile flight over open sea to Howland, a tiny Pacific island. Howland was only 2 miles long and a half-mile wide. It had a newly built runway. Amelia planned to refuel on the island, go on to Hawaii, and then home. After a three-day delay, they left for Howland.

A ship called the *Itasca* was assigned to guide the Electra to Howland using radio and black smoke signals. For unknown reasons, Amelia used weak radio frequencies, and the *Itasca* was unable to read her messages. Again and again the ship's crew tried to guide them to the island, but without success. They begged her to change radio frequencies, but Amelia didn't seem to hear them. Finally they received a message: "We must be on you but cannot see you... Only half-hour's gas left."

No one knows what happened. Search planes and ships were sent out, but Amelia and Noonan were never found.

She was a full-time pilot for only ten years, but Amelia Earhart was an influential pilot and role model. She showed the world that women could be as adventurous and daring as men.

Glossary

Acclaimed - highly praised.

Adventurous - having a taste for adventure.

Altimeter - a gauge on an airplane that shows how high in the air it is.

Altitude - a measure of how high something is.

Autogiro - an aircraft made in the 1930s that was the first kind of helicopter. It had two engines, one on the front like a regular plane, and one on the top with very long propellers so it could take off without moving forward. It was invented by Juan de la Cierva of Spain.

Churned - in constant motion.

Continent - a very large piece of land—there are seven continents in the world.

Credit - praise or recognition for doing something.

Distinguished - famous and well thought of.

Equator - the line that marks the widest part of the Earth. It separates the northern hemisphere from the southern hemisphere.

Frequency - in radio, a broadcast signal with a sending and receiving channel. To listen to someone who is sending signals on a frequency, you have to receive the signals on that same frequency.

Gainful - successful or profitable.

Helicopter - an aircraft that has one large propeller on top for moving around and one in back for stability.

Historic - important to the progress of a technology or an idea.

Instruments - gauges in an airplane. If a pilot is "flying on instruments" it means that the view out of the window is blocked by clouds or smoke, and the pilot has to rely on the instruments in order to tell how high the plane is and how close it is to an airport.

Interfere - to affect or prevent something from happening with unwanted attention.

London - the capital of England.

Navigator - someone who keeps track of where a plane or boat is going.

Nevertheless - in spite of.

New Guinea - a large island just north of Australia.

Oakland - A city in California near San Francisco.

Occupation - job.

Outfitted - equipped with. Extras are added to something to make it more useful.

Parachute - a large piece of material, like silk, that is used to slow something down when it is falling from a great height.

Permanently - without changing.

Pontoons - big hollow structures.

Predicted - in weather, forecasted or guessed at.

Publicity - attention from the media.

Runway - a long, flat paved strip of land where airplanes take off and land.

Singapore - a small country in Southeast Asia.

Talent - a special ability to do something well.

Volunteer - working without being paid, usually for a good cause.